Crossing Over
TO A CLOSER WALK WITH GOD

GRANT CRARY

Fairdale Publishing

Crossing Over
TO A CLOSER WALK WITH GOD
By Grant Crary

Copyright © 2016 Grant Crary. All rights reserved
ISBN: 978-0-9982243-0-5

Cover Design: Kristen Ide

Bible references:
All scripture is taken from the New King James Version. Copyright © 1982 by Thomas Nelson, Inc. All rights reserved. Used by permission.

Printed in the United States of America

Published by:
Fairdale Publishing
www.fairdalepublishing.com

No part of this publication may be reproduced, stored in a retrieval system, or transmitted in any form, or by any means, electronic, mechanical, including photocopy, recording, or by any informational storage and retrieval system, without the prior, written permission of the publisher. Please direct permission requests and other correspondences to Fairdale Publishing at www.fairdalepublishing.com.

This book is dedicated to my wife, Jillian, who has been my friend and companion throughout our life together. Her wisdom, kindness, encouragement, and love for the Lord are a priceless blessing.

Contents

	Introduction vii
1.	Crossing Over 1
2.	It All Depends on Our Heart.. 7
3.	What is Spiritual Maturity? 13
4.	How Can We Determine Whether We Are Maturing? 21
5.	The Ways of God 31
6.	A Love for the Truth 39
7.	Prayer and Bible Study 45
8.	The Use of our Time 53
9.	Expanding by Contracting 61
10.	The Example of the Apostle John 69
11.	The Keys 77
12.	Does God Know My Name? 81

Introduction

From the beginning of my Christian walk, I could see in the Bible examples of men and women who had a close relationship with God, and I knew that there was much more available for me than what I was experiencing. There is, of course, always more for us throughout our life because of the unfathomable riches of God. The question is though, how do we grow spiritually and experience a closer relationship? Can we become like Abraham and Moses and be called a friend of God? What is required on our part?

There have been certain truths that have been particularly important in my own spiritual life and growth, and I made notes on them so that I could pass them on to others. My notes tend to be brief, something to jog my memory, and I realized that it would be more helpful to another person if I expanded them into a readable form. That is how this book came about, not because I set out to write a book but from a desire to pass on specific lessons that have been important to me.

In order to keep the chapters short and make it easier for the reader to grasp the main point, the book does not elaborate on the topics at great length. Also, this is not intended to be a comprehensive study on Christian growth or even on any of the specific topics. Instead, the book covers certain lessons that have been important in my own life, things that the Lord has impressed upon me. Understanding them and applying them has blessed me greatly.

    I believe that God places within us a desire to know Him and that it is His desire to have a close relationship with us too. It is my prayer that these lessons will be of value to the readers and that developing our relationship with the Lord will become the most important thing in our life.

CHAPTER ONE

Crossing Over

The apostle Paul wrote that the journey of the children of Israel from Egypt to Canaan is an example for us in our Christian walk (1 Corinthians 10:6). One aspect of the journey that we observe is the propensity for the people to contemplate returning to Egypt when some difficulty arose. When there was no water or they became tired of the food, they complained and talked about how good life was in Egypt and how it would be better to return. They seemed to forget that in Egypt they were harshly-treated slaves! They also forgot the miraculous deliverance that God had brought about through the ten plagues and at the Red Sea, demonstrating His loving care and providing a basis for faith for future events. Although they were happy to follow Moses and keep the Law most of the time, moving forward in obedience to the command of God was not a settled issue in their hearts. Consequently, they were prone to wavering.

Everything changed when the people crossed the Jordan and entered Canaan, the Promised Land. No longer did they look back to Egypt, no longer did they talk about how good things used to be. Instead, they looked forward, united under Joshua to defeat the inhabitants and take possession of the territory that God had promised. Which required greater courage, discipline, and obedience… travelling through the wilderness with its hardships or going to war against superior forces to drive them out? I'm not sure of the answer because both were challenging. Both had aspects of danger, both required trusting God for a favorable outcome when the circumstances were against them. However, the one aspect that stands out as being so very different is the mindset of the people. Once they had crossed the Jordan, they only looked forward.

Likewise for us, there is a sense in which we have to "cross over" with regards to certain things. For example, alcohol was a huge problem in my family and shortened the lives of several of my relatives. I became a Christian when I was eighteen and about two years later I received prayer to break that hold in my life. God certainly met me and alcohol has never been a problem for me or my children but it was in other family members of my generation and in their children too.

I began to be appalled by the destruction that alcohol brought to my family so I decided that I would limit my consumption. I wanted to be a good Christian but at the same time I wanted to retain acceptance in the family. Cutting back to a minimum seemed to be the logical solution. One day I realized that if I was to truly help the family, I had to set a standard that they could see and merely reducing my consumption was not visible to them. So, I decided to stop drinking altogether. This resulted in a storm of opposition for me because I was now regarded as an embarrassment to the family, but I had made my decision. Like Israel at the Jordan, I had "crossed over" and left appearances behind. The opposition was severe but in other ways things became easier. My position was clear, the line was no longer blurred. My Christianity stood for something that directed my life, not just some nice appendage.

Interestingly, as time went by the family's attitude toward me changed as they became resigned to the fact that I would not compromise my stance. Not one of them altered their own drinking habits but when a problem arose they would turn to me for advice. I was in my early-to-mid-twenties, at the beginning of my adult life, while their ages ranged from late forties upward, so one would not expect them to seek advice from someone with such limited life experiences. Nevertheless, I was regarded as the fountain of wisdom and knowledge in the family, no doubt because my wife and I had stability in our home and life.

There are times in our life, when we have to "cross over." We have to make a commitment to change some behavior or to exercise faith in some direction, but we feel secure in familiar surroundings so stepping forward can be uncomfortable. If we are to grow in God though, stepping forward is essential, and the truth is that it should not be regarded as a hardship for us. The apostle John wrote that the commandments of the Lord are not burdensome (1 John 5:3) and the more our relationship with Him grows, the more we delight to please Him. The apostle Paul is a good example of this. Prior to his conversion he was a Pharisee which meant that he was accustomed to privileges, respect, and even power. There were probably financial benefits too. However, Paul wrote that although he had suffered the loss of all things, he considered it as refuse compared to the relationship with the Lord that he now enjoyed (Philippians 3:8). To Paul, absolutely nothing compared to the "excellence of the knowledge of Christ Jesus." It is true that as we grow closer to the Lord, Paul's experience becomes our own too.

The enormous blessings of a close relationship with the Lord cannot be obtained without crossing over at various times in our life. At some point, we have to decide whether we want to retain certain things that we have come to realize are unfruitful, or whether we will remove them. We have to decide on the things that hold priority for our time and energies, whether having favor with God is more important than favor with people, or whether we will invest the time to develop our relationship. In this regard, I have found three important things to be true:

(1) God is certainly a rewarder of those who diligently seek Him (Hebrews 11:6).
(2) The rewards that He has for us exceed our expectations.
(3) He has rewards for us that we never imagined.

I have observed that true men and women of God all pay a price in terms of the things of this world. They don't do all the things that others do and often are misunderstood, even maligned by those who have other standards. Their life is disciplined, they maintain a righteous behavior that does not vary from day-to-day or circumstance-to-circumstance, their favorite subjects to discuss revolve around the things of God. It is not an act that they have to carry out, it is simply who they have become. They consider themselves greatly blessed because the Lord shares secrets with them, and gives them insights that most others do not see. His presence in their daily life is so enjoyable, so constant. They regard the cost as a means to an end, not something missing from their life, and they would not trade what God has given them for anything because it is precious.

When General Eisenhower and his military team were about to launch the invasion of Europe in June 1944, what became known as D-Day, they faced a serious problem. The weather was so adverse that a crossing of the English Channel was impossible and Erwin Rommel, a prominent German general who was the main architect of the defenses on the northern French coast, actually left France to celebrate his wife's birthday, certain that the invasion could not be undertaken. However, a meteorologist told Eisenhower and his men that he believed there would be a window in a couple of days when the weather would abate sufficiently to enable the invasion to take place. The conditions would not be ideal but a crossing might be possible.

Eisenhower was faced with a momentous decision. To launch the invasion and have it fail would be an unmitigated disaster with substantial loss of troops and equipment, and weather forecasting has never been an exact science so he could not be certain of the meteorologist's prediction. On the other hand, the tides would not be favorable for another month which would give the Germans extended time to prepare the defenses. They might even determine which beaches had been selected by the Allies for landing, taking away all element of surprise. Also, what would he do with all the troops and armaments for a month? When the order is given to bring a substantial military force forward, it is not easy to change course.

As we know, Eisenhower decided to invade and it was successful. To do so, he had to place his eggs into one single basket and cross the channel to land in France. Similarly, we have to place our eggs in a single basket too. We have to determine that we will trust God, that developing a close relationship with Him is worth more than everything else, that any risks associated with this walk are paltry by comparison. We have to decide that we will cross over wherever He leads.

It is my hope and prayer that the thoughts in this book will be stepping stones to help those who read it in their spiritual walk. May we all be found to be good and faithful servants, walking in the fear of the Lord, and experiencing the associated blessings that He grants so liberally.

CHAPTER TWO

It All Depends on Our Heart

What do we really want? Really, at the bottom of our heart? Often, that is not an easy question to answer. We tend to present what we believe to be the right answer, what we think we should be saying, but when we examine our heart closely we may find that some other thing is more important to us. The heart of man is certainly deceptive (Jeremiah 17:9). There are times when we may say, for example, that we want to follow God no matter where He leads but when some obstacle or inconvenience arises we realize that our heart wants certain other things as well. These other things compete for pre-eminence in our heart. For example, we might truly desire to serve the Lord but when He calls us to a role that is obscure and perhaps abasing, we find that our heart also desires position and recognition, causing us to buck at the course He has set before us. Sometimes we do not even realize that an element of pride or selfishness exists within us but God sets up the circumstances to bring it to the surface.

Jesus spoke of this very condition in the Parable of the Sower. There was seed that fell amongst thorns which choked the growth of the seed (Luke 8:14). We should note that there is no criticism of the seed in this parable. The problem was the soil where the seed landed. In this instance, both the seed and the thorns grew together and the thorns prevented the seed from producing fruit to maturity. The thorns are described as being cares, riches, and pleasures of life. None of these things are necessarily wrong. The fact that one has cares could be founded in a sense of responsibility, and Proverbs tells us that it is the love of riches, not riches themselves that are at the root of evil. Further, did not God give us things in this world for our enjoyment? Therefore, cares, riches, and pleasures are not wrong in themselves. It is when we become overly absorbed by them that they become an obstacle to spiritual growth.

Here lies a test for us. Can we truly ask God if something in our life has become a thorn bush or do we push the question to one side just in case God views it that way and we need to change? Is our desire to grow spiritually and become closer to the Lord greater than our desire to continue in a certain lifestyle? The question reveals what is in our heart; whether or not pleasing Him and growing closer to Him is not just important but is truly the most important thing to us. We have to be brutally honest with our answers.

It is usually not the things in themselves that become thorns but our attitude toward them and the place that we assign to them in our life. The fact that something is not wrong in itself becomes an excuse to continue to devote time, energy and finances into pursuing it excessively, when all the while God is saying to us that it has become a thorn bush that is choking out the progress of the good seed that He wants to develop.

Often these issues are not obvious. For example, there was a man named Demas who was a companion of the apostle Paul.

The apostle referred to him as his "fellow laborer" in his letter to Philemon. However, something went terribly wrong. When writing his final letter, which was addressed to Timothy, Paul says that "Demas has forsaken me, having loved this present world" (2 Timothy 4:10). We are not told specifically what Demas did or just why he left Paul, but obviously there was some thorn bush in his heart that choked out his good works and caused him to put other things first. Demas had traveled with Paul, enduring many hardships and had been part of the founding of churches amongst Gentile people. There must have been many wonderful experiences and occasions where the hand of God was miraculously displayed, not to mention the joy of seeing lives transformed. Yet there was something in the heart of Demas that emerged and caused him to change his course. Somewhere he lost sight of eternal values, his heart being drawn aside to something else that attracted him. We don't know if he later came back to the Lord, but it is a sobering lesson for us to realize that someone who had been privileged to be part of such amazing things may have ultimately lost his salvation. It should lead us to say with King David, "Search me Oh God.... and see if there is any wicked way in me." (Psalm 139:23-24). We need to ask the Lord to reveal our heart to us lest we lose our fervor or, worse still, lose our way.

The book of Proverbs warns us, "Keep your heart with all diligence, for out of it spring the issues of life (Proverbs 4:23). "Diligence" means "careful and continued hard work." The definition implies persistence and consistency, being in it for the long haul. We tend to be attracted to people with charismatic personalities rather than those who are less exciting but reliable. However, in the Christian life, reliability is a commendable virtue. Plodding along is better than flashes of brilliance.

Some years ago, I built a concrete block retaining wall and the Lord taught me some important lessons in the process. Once the foundation was poured and the construction of the actual wall was about to start, I wondered if I had done the right thing. I had never built a wall before and the individual blocks seemed so small. I thought it would take me the rest of my life! (Well, not really, but the task did seem daunting). The construction took four long, summer days and I learnt that by consistently performing small tasks I could complete a large project. Each block was relatively small but, by laying one after another, I built the wall.

We could say that building the wall was an exercise in diligence – careful and continued hard work. The wall demonstrated to me that substantial goals can be accomplished by consistently making the right decisions in relatively small matters. By laying one small block after another, I completed a large project. In a spiritual sense, if we consistently do the right thing, even in small matters, our lives are shaped to become the man or woman that God intended. However, if we fail to make good decisions in the small things, we leave our heart open to desiring the wrong things and we will almost certainly miss God's plan for us. That wall was perfectly level and perfectly straight but imagine how it would have looked had I left out some blocks periodically. Aside from the strange appearance, it would have been weaker because I could not have properly filled the cells of the blocks with concrete as is a necessary aspect of the construction.

Another important aspect of spiritual growth is how we handle trials. It is in trials that we learn about God's faithfulness and our trusting Him is an essential ingredient to our growth. I am reminded of a man who shared how he was looking at a snow-capped mountain one day. He was standing at the base which was bathed in sunlight. The upper portion of the mountain was also bathed in sunlight. However, thick cloud covered the central portion. The Lord spoke to him and said that the mountain represented his spiritual walk. The highest points of the mountain were blessed with the presence of God, but to get there he would have to pass through the clouded areas. Similarly, in our lives we have to pass through difficulties to come out into blessing. We have to hold the attitude of the three Israelites who were threatened with the fiery furnace for not worshiping the image that King Nebuchadnezzar had set up. Their response was that God was able to deliver them, but if He did not they still would not worship the king's image (Daniel 3:16-18). Their response is very insightful because they stated that God was well able to deliver them. However, if He should choose not to do so, that was okay with them too. They were committed to doing the right thing, regardless of the consequences. Their eyes were firstly on eternal, spiritual values, not other things, even the preservation of their lives. No thorn bushes there!

Our heart will determine our path. Will we walk the right path? And how far along that path are we willing to walk? Many of us start well but then stall at a certain point. This is because we do not place the highest value on eternal matters…coming to know God closely, being obedient in all things, being changed more and more into His likeness. Instead, other things occupy too great a place in our heart or we are not willing to follow God in a time of difficulty.

Some things in life are mutually exclusive. One day when Jesus was teaching about how to handle money, He stated a principle that applies to all aspects of life. He said that we cannot serve two masters because we will not be able to love both (Matthew 6:24). If we are to go further with God we have to choose where to place our love. Will it be in the highest things of God or in some mixture at a lower plane? Does our desire for the highest things outweigh our reticence to experience the cost that comes with attaining them? Will that cost cause us to consciously or unconsciously stop short of all that God intended for us? So it comes down to the simple question, "What do we really want?"

Further discussion:
- What things that are not necessarily bad in themselves, might be preventing us from reaching spiritual maturity because they occupy too large a place in our life?
- Consider an area in your life where the principle of building a block wall could be applicable to accomplishing a goal. This could be a task or a change in a behavior where small changes, consistently applied, will add up over time.
- Why would we not want to pass through clouded areas of life when there is an opportunity for greater blessing at the end?

CHAPTER THREE

What is Spiritual Maturity?

It is a principle of life that things grow. They usually do not keep growing forever but they grow until they have attained to full maturity. For example, people are not born at their final height but continue to grow well into their teen's and sometimes their twenty's until they reach their full height as a mature person and their growth stops. In fact, if something does not grow it is indicative of a problem. I see this principle in a grapefruit tree that is in my yard. This tree produces very large, sweet grapefruit which are delicious to eat but each of those grapefruit starts out green and quite small. I look forward to eating the grapefruit but I do not attempt to do so when they are green. Instead, I wait until the fruit has matured because while it is delicious when mature, it is unpleasant to eat when green.

Growth is also imperative in our spiritual life. We should continue to grow throughout all our days because God is so perfect and so complete that there will always be room for improvement.

Therefore, we have two important questions to consider; (1) What constitutes spiritual maturity, and (2) How can we determine whether we are growing or not?

When a person receives Christ and becomes a Christian there is evidence that attests to their having had a true conversion. The person will experience peace within themselves, resulting from the forgiveness of sins and the restoration of relationship with God. They will also experience changes in their life with sinful behaviors being replaced by righteous ones. Others will notice these changes too. In a true conversion, there is ample evidence of the presence of Christ having entered that person's life.

However, a person who receives Christ must go on to maturity. Sometimes we confuse maturity with other things. For example, if a person has a ministry in which people are being saved through their preaching or healed through their prayers, does that mean that they are spiritually mature? The answer is, "Maybe." Generally speaking, God develops ministry abilities in people as they mature, and typically that ministry becomes more and more effective in conjunction with their growth in their walk with Him. But this is not always the case. Sometimes we see God do amazing things through a new Christian who has simple faith and a love in their heart to serve Him. Also, someone who has grown in their walk and ministry may have a moral failing so even though the ministry continues, there comes a time when that failing is exposed, usually bringing the ministry to an abrupt end. I have seen that there is a human tendency to try to cover over the failing so that the ministry is not damaged, but God is more concerned with the person's standing with Him and will expose the failing to bring correction to the person.

Generally, we would expect an older person to be more spiritually mature than a younger person because the older person has had more time to learn from God and glean from life's experiences. Again, generally speaking, that is correct but it is not necessarily so. There are younger people who have matured beyond their years, like the Apostle Paul's spiritual son, Timothy, who held great responsibility in the First Century church. Similarly, there are older people who have not progressed very far in spite of being churchgoers for much of their lives, evidenced by inconsistencies in their behaviors and shortcomings in their concept of God. An example is the counsellors of Job. They were three older men who did not have the understanding of a fourth man who was much younger. So while age and the length of time one has been a Christian are usually relevant to a person's level of spiritual maturity, it is clear that this is not always the case.

If spiritual maturity is not necessarily related to age or spiritual gifting, what should we look for in a person's life as evidence of progression toward maturity? A good place to start would be to examine the teachings of Jesus and the apostles to see what they considered important. When we do so, we find that a consistent theme is character. Jesus taught about character throughout His ministry. A good example is the Sermon on the Mount and another is His parables. His rebukes of the Pharisees and religious leaders were always over their adherence to the set of rules that they had established as being the yardstick for righteous behavior, rather than true character issues. For example, in Matthew 23:23-24, He commends them for tithing but rebukes them for neglecting the more important matters of justice, mercy, and faith. He calls them "blind guides," people who were leading others but did not themselves know where they were going. They majored in works instead of character. They kept rules that they thought made them righteous but actually they were prideful, greedy, controlling, and judgmental, and because of these character shortcomings they could not see truth.

Similarly, the apostles taught about character and right living. Their letters contain instruction in practical matters such as the behavior in church meetings and qualifications for elders and deacons, but without a doubt the overriding instructions pertain to character. In fact, none of them mince their words when writing about church people who live ungodly lives.

Maturity in the Bible is often described in terms of three broad stages. Jesus talked about bearing fruit, more fruit, and much fruit through abiding in Him and being pruned by the Father (John 15:1-5). In the Parable of the Sower, He talked about good soil that would bear a crop of thirty-fold, sixty-fold, and one hundred-fold (Matthew 13:8). In the book of Revelation, we read that those who are with the Lord are called, chosen, and faithful (Revelation 17:14). And the apostle John, writing to saints in the churches that he oversaw, categorized them as children, young men, and fathers (1 John 2:12-14). John addressed the stages of growth in terms of men but the same is true for women. To understand Christian maturity better, we shall consider John's categorization of the stages of growth as it provides detail that helps us understand. And to reiterate, the comments regarding Children, Young Men, and Fathers are stages of growth that apply equally to women as well as to men.

Firstly, his description of children is that they have known the Father and that their sins are forgiven. In life, children have limited knowledge and understanding, but also limited responsibilities. This is because their capabilities have not been developed. In a spiritual sense, these are people who know the basics; they have been saved, their sins are forgiven, they are going to Heaven, and that God is good, merciful, and just. At this stage in life they know more *about* God than they know Him through experience.

Young men, however, have considerably greater capabilities. John says that they are strong, that they know the Word of God, and they overcome the devil. These attributes speak of a significant level of spiritual development. These are solid Christians who walk in faith and minster in the power of the Holy Spirit. They are capable of starting works, leading congregations, teaching the truths of Scripture, and are well grounded in their walk. They can be compared to natural young men whose intelligence is developed and their physical abilities enable them to do most anything. We see this in the military where young soldiers pilot aircraft, drive tanks, and perform many demanding tasks involving expensive, sophisticated equipment. Although still young, they have attained to a level of considerable ability and the same is true in the spiritual sense regarding those that John describes as young men.

So what separates fathers from young men? Naturally speaking, fathers may have developed their physical and intellectual abilities beyond those of young men but the differences are usually not great, or at least not as great as the difference between a child and a young man. What makes a father stand out is the wisdom gained through experience. Fathers have learned important lessons over time, often through their own mistakes, but also through the experiences of life. Consequently, they are able to provide direction and wise oversight to others. They have acquired understanding as well as knowledge. It is one thing to have knowledge but much of this can be gained through study. Understanding, however, comes with experience, and while knowledge is essential, understanding will take us further.

Similarly in a spiritual sense, a father has understanding and can provide wise direction. John says that fathers know God. This is not a head knowledge, nor a superficial knowledge as is the case with an acquaintance, but a deep relationship where the Christian has come to truly know how God thinks and what He is like because these things have been his or her experience. This cannot be gained academically but only through consistently following the Lord over a lengthy period of time.

It also involves passing through trials because it is in trials that our faith is tested and proven. Trials reveal what we really believe. In difficult situations, we have to make decisions as to whether we will trust God, whether we really believe that He is who the Bible says He is, whether we will continue to be true to Him even if the circumstances do not change or work out how we would like, and whether it is true that "all things work together for good to those who love God and are called according to His purpose" (Romans 8:28). We find that He has His own timetable, that He is able to change things that we cannot change, and that in the end He truly is faithful, but these things have to be our experience. Until we pass through a trial, they are only theory.

We can understand what is required to become a father from a passage in the book of Jeremiah. In chapter 9, verses 23-24, we are instructed not to be proud if we have wisdom (in this case, better understood as intellect and learning) hold a position of power, or are wealthy. It is not that there is anything inherently wrong with these things, and in fact they are all actually commendable if God is placed first in our lives. However, Jeremiah tells us that what should be truly important to us is to understand and know the Lord, which is how John describes a father.

The passage goes on to summarize the key elements regarding God that we have to come to understand. Firstly, we have to know that He is "the Lord." We have to know that there is none like Him, none possessing His wisdom and power. He is the true Supreme Being, the Lord of all. This will cause us to be very reverential, desiring to live our life in a manner that is pleasing to Him, humble, having confidence in His ability to hear our prayers, having confidence in His great love for us, full of praise and thankfulness. The passage then mentions three characteristics of God which describe the essential elements of His nature; lovingkindness, judgement, and righteousness. God is fully righteous and, in fact,

He is incapable of unrighteousness. He exercises judgment as well as lovingkindness, two qualities which represent the opposite ends of the spectrum of His character. We must seek to have the Holy Spirit work these qualities into our own lives so that we become more and more like Him.

Something that I have found in my Christian life is that God does not always reveal to us blessings that He has in store until it is His timing. Moreover, often these blessings are things that we would not have thought of, or would not have considered to be available to us. I believe that God has things that are very wonderful for us, "hidden riches of secret places" as Isaiah describes them, but they are found by passing through dark places (Isaiah 45:3). We have to grow in our understanding of God and in our faith and trust in Him. We have to be sure in our hearts that He is precisely who the Bible describes Him, full of virtue, full of love for us.

We see then, that achieving Christian maturity is coming to truly know the Lord and in order to truly know Him, we must be people of character. Having a close relationship with someone is dependent upon compatibility, and to be compatible with God we must be people of character because His character is impeccable. The prophet Amos referred to the necessity of being compatible with God when he asked the rhetorical question, "Can two walk together, unless they are agreed?" (Amos 3:3). Jesus made the statement that it would be the pure in heart who would qualify to see God (Matthew 5:8). If we want to become spiritually mature, a father as John puts it, we have to have the character of God worked into our lives so that we can know Him.

Therefore, it is important that we consider what is in the heart rather than external appearances because that is how God looks at us. God can most certainly use our natural abilities but these must be subjugated to His will and not be the measure of our spirituality. Saul was rejected by God for his disobedience but the underlying reason was that the approval of man mattered more to him than the approval of God (1 Samuel 15:24, 30). The heart of David, on the other hand, was precisely the opposite. When he sinned in the matter of Bathsheba and Uriah, all that mattered to him was the restoration of his relationship with God (Ps 51:10-11). This is the fundamental reason why David succeeded and Saul did not.

So being spiritually mature is about having character. Maturity is not measured by skills, age, personality, or any other such factor. It is about becoming like Him.

Further discussion:
- What is the advantage of having understanding regarding a certain subject compared to having knowledge of it?
- Trials are not pleasant and it is human nature to try to get out of them quickly, but what are the benefits of trials?
- What do you really think God is like? Is your concept of Him in accordance with the Bible?

CHAPTER FOUR

How Can We Determine Whether We Are Maturing?

In the previous chapter, we considered what constitutes spiritual growth and maturity, and concluded that God sees things differently from us. We tend to look at the things that we see, such as abilities and personality. However, God makes His evaluation using a different yardstick.

There is a good example of this in the account of the selection of David to be the next king of Israel. God had rejected King Saul and told the prophet Samuel to go to the house of Jesse where He had found a man with a heart like His own. That in itself is a very significant statement. God wanted a man who would see things the way He saw them and when we look at certain instances in David's life, such as his sparing of Saul not once but twice, we can understand why he was so dear to the heart of God. Although Saul had obviously departed from following God's ways, he had come to the throne by the appointment of God, not through some unjust takeover or even through succession. David was not about to overrule God's decision by taking Saul's life, regardless of how that would benefit him personally. David must have reasoned that if God wanted to remove Saul from office He was very capable of doing so, just as He had appointed him to that position in the first place.

When Samuel went to Jesse's house where God would select one of Jesse's son's, he first saw Eliab and immediately thought that this was the Lord's man. Eliab was the oldest, something that would make him the most likely choice in his day, and he must have been a tall, strong, handsome man with a presence about him because Samuel said, "Surely the Lord's anointed is before Him!" (1 Samuel 16:6). We can picture Samuel stepping forward with the flask of oil in his hand, ready to pronounce Eliab as the future king, when the Lord stopped him. The Lord said to Samuel, "Do not look at his appearance or his physical stature, because I have refused him. For the Lord does not see as man sees; for man looks at the outward appearance, but the Lord looks at the heart" (1 Samuel 16:7). As we know, eventually David was brought before Samuel and the Lord told the prophet that this was His man. David was the youngest, still a teenager, and obviously not regarded in the same class as his brothers because Jesse did not even think to bring him before Samuel until Samuel asked if there was another son. But God looked at the heart, not the outward appearance.

Although David was still a youth, God saw in him a desire to know God and to walk in His ways. This was the yardstick that God used for his selection, not the external attributes of age, appearance, and rank. God knew that possessing a heart like this, David would become a mature man of God.

So what are the qualities that are indicative of maturity? There are a number of places in the Bible that address maturity and they are all in some way related to character. True maturity is becoming more like Jesus so the qualities that we see in Him need to become our qualities too. One section of the Bible that lists these qualities is the Fruit of the Spirit, found in Galatians 5:22-23. These nine fruit are the nature of the Holy Spirit and are to become our nature as we grow closer to the Lord and become a reflection of Him.

Jesus taught His disciples to distinguish between good, sound people (sheep) and those that are really wolves in sheep's clothing, even though the wolves may look and sound like sheep. He said that we can distinguish them by the fruit of their lives (Matthew 7:15-20). Just as a tree produces fruit that is a reflection of the type of tree (apple, peach, almond…) so too does the fruit in people's lives reflect the type of person that that they are (kind, encouraging, bitter, selfish…). We do not judge people in the sense of criticizing or condemning them, but we should show the wisdom to consider the fruit of their lives and the outcome of their ministry and make an appropriate assessment regarding that person. This is inspecting the fruit.

The fruit listed in Galatians are as follows:

- **Love.** Peter, John, and Paul all discuss love and all of them consider it to be the highest quality. Peter listed eight progressive steps to maturity and the last and highest of these is love (2 Peter 1:5-7).

    John wrote, "God is love" (1 John 4:8, 4:16). He also said that "If someone says 'I love God' and hates his brother, he is a liar; for if he does not love his brother whom he has seen, how can he love God whom he has not seen?" (1 John 4:20). The topic of love is covered throughout John's first letter, being mentioned 26 times in just 105 verses.

Paul stated that regardless of what accomplishments, abilities, and sacrifices he might have or make, without love he was a clanging cymbal, of no value, simply nothing (1 Corinthians 13:1-3). Paul was a man whose accomplishments were enormous by any standard, but he knew that love was what really mattered, not his great accomplishments. Love is the fundamental nature of God and it is a fruit that He desires to be developed in us. The essence of love is unselfishness.

- **Joy.** Joy is the result of righteousness and thankfulness. People who harbor unforgiveness, or practice some aspect of sin, or complain continually, may have occasions of happiness in their lives but they will not know the joy of the Lord, certainly not on a consistent basis. The Bible describes this joy as being our strength (Nehemiah 8:10) so it is something that we really need. Disagreeable, bitter people are not easy people to be with but the presence of the Lord, expressed in a joyful disposition, is a most attractive quality.

- **Peace** is also the result of righteousness. We cannot know peace if we are not in a right relationship with the Lord and with others. Our peace will increase as we grow closer to Him. Both peace and joy are rewards from the Lord. Peace is something that people seek, and people who are at peace bring peace into situations.

- **Longsuffering.** This is the ability to endure difficulties for an extended period of time while maintaining a good attitude and increasing in our love for God. It has the effect of softening us without breaking us, removing pride, and making us more understanding of the ways of God. People with this quality have a deep trust in God and there is a stability about them, even in difficult times.

- **Kindness.** Sometimes what people do and say is not kind. What a person says may be true but is it kind to say those things, or is it kind to say them in that manner? Kindness must replace selfishness. A person who is kind thinks of how things affect others rather than themselves.

- **Goodness.** This is having a wholesomeness about us, a purity of heart. It can only be developed by having the fear of the Lord within us to keep us from evil in deed, word, and even in thought. The way we think will translate into how we speak and act, so having thoughts that are good, pure, and wholesome is essential to maturity.

- **Faithfulness.** This is a quality that is diminishing in society today. We must accept our responsibilities and be reliable, trustworthy people, even when we are not being observed, and even if the task has lost its enjoyment and sense of reward.

- **Gentleness.** David wrote of the Lord that His "gentleness has made me great" (Psalm 18:35). We tend to regard gentleness as being a sign of weakness but God sees it differently. In some versions of the Bible, the word is translated as "meekness" and it is the quality of having strength under control, being able to resist fighting back, like the Lord in the time of intense provocation in His trials and crucifixion.

- **Self-control.** We need to be disciplined people, conducting ourselves appropriately and not being prone to outbursts, violence, and foolish behavior. Undisciplined people are not mature people, either in their Christian walk or in other aspects of their life.

Just as a tree produces fruit after its kind, so we as Christian people are to produce fruit that shows the presence of Jesus within us, the fruit of the Spirit. As we become more like Him, the fruit of our life reveals Him within us. These nine fruit have been discussed above only in the briefest of terms and we would do well to ponder each one, evaluating its presence or absence in our lives. Then we should ask the Lord to work these fruit into us so that we can become a reflection of Him.

Another quality that speaks of maturity is wisdom. There is not a person that I have met who was spiritually mature who was not also wise. Wisdom is the correct application of knowledge in a given situation, it is having good judgement and soundness in actions and decisions. Often it is knowing when to speak and when not to speak. It is a quality that enables us to walk though treacherous situations that could be our undoing.

Jesus faced such situations continuously because the religious leaders of His day were constantly trying to trap Him. It is a sad testament to their actions that instead of desiring to know the truth, they were intent on trying to discredit Him. One such instance was when they asked if it was lawful to pay taxes to Caesar. If Jesus answered "Yes," He would alienate Himself from the people because Roman taxation was very unpopular. If He answered "No," He would have been labeled as an opponent of Rome. It was a clever question because no matter how Jesus answered, the Pharisees would have succeeded in their objective because Jesus would have isolated Himself. Or so it seemed. Jesus is the personification of wisdom and His wisdom was about to be displayed. Rather than address the question head-on, He asked for a coin and then asked whose inscription was on it. The answer was Caesar's inscription, to which Jesus replied, "Render therefore to Caesar the things that are Caesar's, and to God the things that are God's." (Matthew 22:15-22). The Pharisees had no comeback, no way to refute His wisdom, and they simply left. Jesus' wisdom enabled Him to handle a situation that could have derailed His ministry.

The Bible has much to say about wisdom, including how we can become wise. It all starts with having the fear of the Lord in our hearts (Proverbs 9:10). It is interesting that the word translated "fear" does indeed mean to be afraid of someone or something. Does this mean that we should live our lives in a state of perpetual terror of a god who is going to judge us and cause us pain and harm if we step out of line? Certainly not! That is a contradiction of countless examples of His love and mercy. The fear of the Lord then, is to have a healthy regard for the adverse consequences of being disobedient to His commands. This is not because He is going to zap us for breaking them but because "By them your servant is warned and in keeping them there is great reward" (Psalm 19:11). One who walks in the fear of the Lord knows that God's commands are given out of His great love for us for our own good and protection in life. To violate them is foolishness, like a sheep straying from the fold and becoming prey to a wolf. Much of the pain and disaster in our lives is the consequence of our own actions that we bring upon ourselves that cause us the pain and disaster.

The fear of the Lord is also described as having a hatred for evil (Proverbs 8:13). If we consider the use of the word "hatred" in this context to mean the opposite of "love" we will understand the statement better. It means that we embrace the opposite of evil, that evil is something that we want no part of in our lives, that the desire of our heart is to live uprightly and blameless, pleasing the Lord. God is good, through and through. Everything He does is right, as Job found after initially having justified himself (Job 42:1-6). Therefore our "hatred" of evil is to side with God and embrace His way, not engaging in any conduct that displeases Him.

There is yardstick for maturity that is very simple to understand and apply… it is what we speak. Jesus told the Pharisees, "Out of the abundance of the heart the mouth speaks" (Matthew 12:34). How we are in our heart will ultimately be expressed by our words, in the words themselves and in the tone and manner that we utter them. If we want to assess the development of the fruit of the Spirit in our lives we can do so by evaluating how we speak.

The apostle James wrote of this in his letter, that if someone does not stumble in word, that person is perfect (James 3:2). The word "perfect" means to be mature. So, a mark of spiritual maturity is having control over one's tongue. The words that come from our mouth should be wholesome, true and sincere. They should be uplifting to the hearers. Our conversation should not be tainted by vulgarity, criticism, put-downs, pride, gossip, bitterness, lies, deceitfulness, or foolish talk. Conversing with us should be something that people welcome because it is wholesome, encouraging, and life-giving. We should be pleasant and uplifting to be around.

It was said of Jesus that He was "full of grace and truth" (John 1:14) and those two words depict how our words should be. They should be sound and reliable, bringing forth truth. We like to talk to people who convey the true situation, not some nonsense that began from a false premise. Truth brings life to us. It may not be what we want to hear, but it will benefit us. Truth sets our thinking on the correct path. However, truth can be hard, just as the Law can be hard. Therefore, our words need the seasoning of grace that adds sweetness. Sometimes truth needs to be conveyed with a great deal of wisdom and this wisdom adds the grace that makes what is said digestible. A person may be unable to receive truth if it is not conveyed with grace.

Does this mean that we should avoid difficult conversations? No, it does not. In life there are many difficult conversations because information has to be relayed and often this information has regard to people. Sometimes we may have to bring correction to an individual and in such a situation, what we say should be spoken clearly because we do not help the other person by avoiding the issue. However, at the same time we should speak with kindness as we seek to help that person overcome the area of weakness.

Our words are very powerful. In Proverbs we read that "Death and life are in the power of the tongue" (Proverbs 18:21). This is an extremely strong statement. It is an interesting phenomenon that people can hurt one-another by their actions and bring great damage to the relationship, but what is even harder to overcome is the words that were spoken. Our words can be like fishhooks that have a barb so that the fish cannot slip off and swim away. The barb of unkind words causes that hurt to remain with us, and speaking too many of those words frequently results in a long-term and sometimes irreversible separation between friends, family, and spouses.

Christian maturity is becoming like Jesus. It is to see things from His perspective, to obey His commands, to honor and please Him in all that we do and say and think. This is the kind of heart that will enable us to become mature.

Further discussion:
- How can we distinguish between evaluating the fruit of someone's life and being critical of them?
- Consider the nine fruit of the Spirit. In what ways will they be visible in our life?
- Look up passages in the Bible that comment on wisdom. If we were to rank the various things that we could desire to have, how high should wisdom be in the list?

CHAPTER FIVE

The Ways of God

This is a very challenging subject to write about because the Bible says that God's ways are "past finding out" (Romans 11:33). It is clear that we cannot fully understand His ways, and indeed only scratch the surface of His great wisdom. I am sure that we will one day understand that everything He does is right and that all His actions will be fully justified, but for now there are things that puzzle us.

Nevertheless, there are certainly things that we are able to understand. In Psalm 103:7 we read, "He made known His ways to Moses, His acts to the children of Israel." Obviously, Moses was a man to whom God gave considerable insight into His ways, but this privilege was not granted to the people. The people saw the things that God did, such as providing manna, a cloud to shelter them from the heat of the day, and a pillar of fire for protection from wild beasts and warmth in the night. Moses, however, lived on a different plane. He not only saw what God did but he understood how God thought. This should be a great motivator for us. If our lives are pleasing to Him, He will grant us insight as to how He thinks and how He views things. We can become people who truly walk with Him.

An example can be seen at the time when the children of Israel listened to the bad report of the ten spies and decided not to go forward into the Promised Land. They complained that it would have been better for them to have died in Egypt or in the wilderness (Numbers 14:2). God declared that they would indeed die in the wilderness for their rebellion and not enter in. He brought a plague which took the lives of the ten spies for their leadership in the distrust of Him. The next morning, the people had a change of heart and said that they wanted to obey God and go forward to enter the Land (Numbers 14:40).

Now we might think that God would be pleased with their repentance and send them forward victorious. We might think, "Praise the Lord, the people have had a change of heart. God will forgive them and now we can go forward to conquer the land." However, Moses understood the ways of God and told them not to go up because they would be defeated. God would not be with them (Numbers 14:41-42). Surely Moses would rather have gone forward than face the prospect of another thirty-eight years in the wilderness, leading a people who murmured and complained continually. However, he could put aside his own wishes and benefits in order to be obedient to God. The people decided to invade anyway and sure enough, they were beaten back. Moses understood how God thought about this situation but the people did not.

We should ask ourselves, what was it that distinguished Moses from the people so that he understood the ways of God? This is a very important question because the Bible record clearly portrays Moses as having an entirely different relationship with God than did the people. Moses and the people all came out of Egypt, travelled the same road in the wilderness, ate the same manna, drank the same water, and endured the same hardships. However, Moses was obedient whereas the people were not. This is essentially the reason why God gave Moses revelation that He would not give to the people.

As we follow the journey of Israel through the wilderness, we see incidents where the people were disobedient. They were constantly complaining, and periodically they would plan to return to Egypt, forgetting their burdens as slaves and remembering only the better variety of food that they ate. In fact, the people failed every test so when it came to believing God and going forward to take the Land they were ill-prepared. The problems actually began all the way back in Egypt because in Ezekiel 20:7-8 and 23:27 we find that the people practiced idolatry in Egypt and brought it with them when they left. They had never dealt thoroughly with this "adulterous" behavior and consequently their spiritual life was one of mixture, sometimes following God and sometimes being disobedient. Moses, on the other hand, was obedient in all things with the exception of the incident when his frustration with the people exploded and he struck the rock twice instead of speaking to it once.

We see then, that obedience to God is a key factor in our being given understanding of His ways. We must love what He loves and hate what He hates. We must hold the same values as does He; we must become like Him, having the fruit of the Spirit worked into our lives. The Roman Centurion understood why Jesus could simply speak a word to heal his servant…it was because Jesus was "a man under authority" (Matthew 8:8-9). Because He lived under the authority of the Father, being obedient in all things, Jesus had the power of the Father available to Him.

Jesus' relationship with the Father was one of perfect union. Throughout His life on Earth, Jesus did the will of the Father, not His own will (John 5:30). He knew the will of the Father and understood His ways. For example, Jesus had an inner circle of disciples, namely Peter, James, and John. James and John were brothers and Peter also had a brother, Andrew, who was a disciple but not part of that inner circle. For some reason not discussed in the Bible, Jesus was not troubled over including one set of brothers but not the other. Excluding Andrew is something that would have greatly troubled us because we would want to treat him fairly and not offend him by excluding him. There is no fault recorded in the Bible regarding Andrew. In fact, he was the one who introduced Peter to Jesus as the Messiah and when Jesus gave His important talk on the Mount of Olives about future events, recorded in Matthew 24, His audience was just the two sets of brothers (Mark 13:3). The reason why Andrew was not part of that inner circle is not at all obvious. We might be concerned about not being fair to Andrew, but Jesus was more concerned about the will of the Father.

Jesus also provided us with the requirements for a similarly close walk. He said, "If anyone serves Me, let him follow Me and where I am, there My servant will be also. If anyone serves Me, him will My Father honor" (John 12:26). This speaks to us of a very close relationship with Jesus and with the Father. Further, He said that keeping His commandments is how we show our love for Him. Our reward will be that Jesus will reveal the Father to us and they will make their dwelling with us (John 14:21, 23). These are promises of unspeakable magnitude and it is wise for us to ponder them deeply. It is our following Him and our obedience to His commands that opens the way for us partake of them.

It is important that we are "transformed by the renewing of our mind" (Romans 12:2) and grow in our understanding of God and His ways. Some people make the mistake of rejecting God, or at least being critical of Him when they do not understand something. The better course is to realize that we may never fully understand some things. However, in everything that we can understand, we find that God is very wise and good, through and through. His love is beyond our comprehension, sending Jesus to suffer and die to provide a way for us to be set free. For Him to engage in wrongdoing is inconsistent with the character and the love that He has demonstrated.

Occasionally, one hears someone talk about how they became angry with God over something. While we can readily identify with being hurt and disappointed, we should not be blaming God. He is incapable of evil, incapable of sin. Instead, we need to know Him better, and we will find Him to be the most wonderful person we could ever wish to know. We should also consider that it is not as if we are in a position to be the judge of Him but rather the reverse. Being angry with Him only reveals that we do not know Him very well.

There are a number of incidents recorded in Scripture where the ways of God are different from our ways. An obvious one is the death and resurrection of Jesus. It is certain that we would not think that the plan of salvation would involve such suffering and humiliation. Rather, we would look for a great leader who could sweep all before him and change everything for our good. However, the plan of God ensured that there could be nothing left open to question by not only providing the way of salvation but by completely fulfilling the Law in the process. The end of the matter is that the name of Jesus is above every other name (Philippians 2:5-11), and when future events were being revealed to John, he saw that Jesus and Jesus alone was considered worthy to open the seals (Revelation 5:1-5).

Let us look at some other examples. In 1 Kings 14 Jeroboam, the king of the northern tribes, is concerned about his young son who is very sick. He decides to send his wife to a prophet to find out if God will heal the boy. The prophet tells his wife that God is going to bring utter disaster on the house of Jeroboam and put an end to all of his descendants so that his line would forever be terminated because he led the nation into idolatry. Then the prophet makes a most unexpected statement. He tells Jeroboam's wife that the boy will die "...because in him there is found something good toward the Lord God" (1 Kings 14:13). If we were not privy to this conversation, what would we think when the child died? We would think that it was such a pity because he was a good boy. Why did he have to die? Why could not God have healed him? However, it was God's respect for the good heart in the boy and His mercy to shield him from the coming judgment on the house of his father that caused God to allow him to die. We would see it as a bad thing whereas actually, it was a good thing.

Please do not think that when a young child dies it is a sign of impending judgment on the family, or that the family must be living sinful lives. The disciples, however, did initially think that way. In John 9, when they met a man who had been blind from birth they asked the Lord if it was the man's sin or the sin of his parents that had caused this sickness. Jesus replied that it had nothing to do with sin but that the works of God would be revealed, and He healed the man. Later, the Pharisees put the man out of the synagogue which was a severe punishment because life revolved around the synagogue. Following this, Jesus met him and revealed to him that He was the Son of God. We might think that it was rough on the man for him to have been born blind and to have lived that way for so many years, just so that the glory of God could be demonstrated in his healing. Also, we might question why he had to suffer being put out of the synagogue, particularly when he had just been healed and had a heart for the Lord. For him in a sense, life went from bad to worse. But Jesus looked at eternal matters.

The end is always what really counts. This man had experienced a difficult life through his blindness and now, in a different way, would continue to do so. Even his parents had been afraid to stand with him. However, he earned the commendation of the Son of God and no doubt his place in Heaven was confirmed by his subsequent obedience to God. We tend to look at how things affect us for this life on earth when we should be looking at eternal values. Our time on earth is typically about eighty years but even if we live to one hundred or more, it is still insignificant compared to eternity. Jesus thought primarily in terms of eternity and that is how we too should think.

Another example is found in the life of Job. In our natural understanding, we would consider God to be grossly unfair to allow Satan to inflict Job so severely. After all, Job was a very righteous man, so much so that God actually considered him to be an example of righteousness in His conversation with Satan. The loss of possessions, children, and his severe illness resulted in Job receiving such an understanding of the glory of God that he was speechless (Job 40:3-5) and was greatly humbled (Job 42:1-6). He came into a wonderful revelation of God (Job 42: 5).

It is interesting that God never apologized to Job for allowing him to suffer so greatly but instead, by revealing His own power and nature, He caused Job to understand more fully his own relative insignificance. Job is listed as being one of the most righteous men in the Old Testament along with Noah and Daniel (Ezekiel 14:14). No doubt his trial qualified him for a higher place in Heaven than would otherwise have been the case because it resulted in a greater degree of purification in his life. God wanted to bless Job and the trial was His means of so doing. Actually, God did not apologize because there was nothing to apologize for. He had given Job an enormous blessing by allowing him to pass through that trial. I am sure that if we could ask Job what he thinks about those hard days he would reply like the apostle Paul that really, it was nothing (Philippians 3:8, 2 Corinthians 4:17), and certainly nothing compared to the blessing that he received from it.

I remember a time when I was out of work and jobs were hard to find. I had interviewed with two companies and really liked the look of the job at one of them but was not so sure about the other. To my disappointment, I was the runner-up for the one that I wanted and when the other company offered me a position I had to accept it. My disappointment grew even greater when it became apparent that this job was a significant step down from my previous duties. I had a young family to support so I needed the income, but I felt so discouraged.

About a year later, I decided to visit the other company to see if there were any openings and to my surprise the doors were closed. The company had gone out of business. As you might imagine, I began to feel much better about my place of work and the business there was growing. I soon received a promotion and another just a few years later, and the things that I learned while working for that company became the foundation for the rest of my career. God's ways were best. When I was looking for a job, He knew how it would work out for both companies and, without my realizing it, He positioned me to gain the experience necessary for my future career.

The ways of God really are different from ours. In His wisdom and foreknowledge He does what is best and right. Unfortunately for us, we can't always see that except in retrospect so it is vital that we learn to trust Him.

Further discussion:
- What qualities does a person need in order to understand that ways of God?
- Why do you think that the Bible says to be transformed by the renewing of our mind, rather than some other means such as forsaking sin?
- Discuss three instances in the Bible, other than those presented in the chapter, where the ways of God were different from our ways.

CHAPTER SIX

A Love for the Truth

In Second Thessalonians chapter two, the apostle Paul writes about the conditions during the reign of the man who we most commonly refer to as the antichrist and who Paul calls the "man of sin," the "son of perdition," and the "lawless one." He talks about the rise to prominence of this world leader who is energized by Satan himself and exercises considerable spiritual power, working "signs and lying wonders with all unrighteousness deception." Then Paul tells why those who are perishing are deceived by these signs and lying wonders... it is because they do not have a love for the truth (v10).

We might have thought the people would be deceived because they lacked the necessary education, or because they were very young in the Lord and did not have sufficient experience to distinguish between the true and the false. Perhaps it could be the miraculous nature of the signs performed by this man and other emissaries of Satan which lead people to think that the signs must be from God. No, the reason was within the hearts of the individuals themselves. They did not have a love for the truth.

In His discourse on the Mount of Olives shortly before going to the cross, the Lord talked much about the deception that would result from the impressive signs that false prophets would perform. He said that they would be so impressive that if it were possible, even the elect of God would be deceived (Matthew 24:24). This tells us that the workings of Satan through his servants will be very great indeed and that it may be easier to be deceived than to not be deceived. However, the elect will discern the difference.

Clearly then, having a love for the truth is a matter of great importance. So what does it mean to have a love for the truth? Let us look at two aspects:

(1) The first is the truth of the Scripture, the Bible, God's Word. Simply put, we have to live according to the precepts and teachings declared in this Book. We cannot pick and choose which ones we like and will follow, and avoid or ignore those that we don't like. There is a human tendency to find a way to justify anything that we want to do, even if it can't really be justified. We cannot have a heart like that. There must be a settled issue in our heart that we want to please the Lord in all our ways or else we might find a way to interpret Scripture to suit our position and fall into deception.

I remember once talking to a Christian leader who had divorced his wife after having been married for many years. I have no doubt that the woman was difficult at times, but there were no actual Biblical grounds for divorcing her. She was willing to continue to be his wife, and having lived together for so long, their separating was a tragedy. The man wanted me to believe that he did in fact have Biblical grounds for the divorce and proceeded to present an interpretation of a relevant passage of Scripture that was stretched to such a degree of distortion that it made absolutely no sense at all. No reasonable person could possibly have thought that the passage could hold the meaning that this man wanted it to have.

I think that in his heart the man knew that he should not have divorced his wife but instead of admitting that he had transgressed he sought to justify his action. Not too long afterward, he committed another transgression in a second relationship and followed this by a third, all of which he was able to justify in his own mind. A man who had once walked uprightly with God and blessed many by his ministry had now twisted Scripture to justify himself, and taken a series of actions that were not pleasing to God. All the while, he continued to attend church and tried to be accepted into leadership. The path was one of deception and the entrance to the deception was his disobedience to the truth instead of loving it. I am certain that had he been willing from the beginning to acknowledge that he had been wrong to divorce his wife, he would never have had to justify his action and consequently he would not have been deceived. He may even have been restored into ministry.

(2) The second aspect has to do with being truthful in the things that we say. We need to be honest and not tell lies, and while that seems to be obvious, many of us do indeed tell lies from time-to-time. It can become a way of life and there are people who are dishonest even when there is no reason to lie. It just becomes a habit and inevitably, one lie leads to another because it is necessary to cover up the first lie. There follows a terrible downward spiral and it does not take long for that person to develop a reputation for being dishonest, often affecting friendships.

There is also another aspect of being truthful in our conversation that is very important. I will illustrate it with an embarrassing example. One day, my boss instructed me to contact a man, who I will call Bill, who worked for the company in a different state, and ask him to provide some information. However, I completely forgot to contact him. A few days later, my boss asked me if I had heard from Bill and I answered by saying that I had not. Now what I said to my boss was perfectly true... I had not heard from Bill.

However, there was a simple reason why and that was because I had not contacted him in the first place. By my answer, I created a false impression that Bill had failed to come through with the information. My "truthful" answer was in fact deceitful. I was horrified that I had given such an answer and I did quickly set the matter straight and rescued Bill's reputation. The incident greatly troubled me and it actually proved to be very beneficial because it caused me to be keenly aware of deceptiveness in what I say. It left me determined to be very careful, not only to be truthful but also not to be deceitful. Having a love for the truth entails being fully truthful. To provide some of the facts but leave out others in order to create a false impression is being deceitful and does not stem from a heart that has a love for the truth.

We should note that in being truthful, we should also be wise. For example, if a friend has purchased some article such as an item of clothing that he/she is very excited about, and you think it looks awful, it is wisdom to find something complimentary to say about it and not express your precise opinion. Your taste is different from your friend's, so the fact that you do not like the item does not necessarily mean that it is actually bad. Nothing is gained from unnecessarily causing an offence.

We should ask ourselves what God thinks of lies and deceitfulness. After all, it is His opinion that counts in the end. The short answer is that He hates such behavior and so we should too. The following are some passages of Scripture that reveal God's heart in the matter:

- Psalm 24:4 Those who want to ascend the hill of the Lord must not swear deceitfully.

- Psalm 32:2 A person who has no deceit in his spirit is described as being blessed.

- Proverbs 12:20 Deceit is in the hearts of those who plot evil.

- Isaiah 53:9 Speaking of the Lord, this passage says that no deceit was in His mouth.

- Mark 7:22 Deceit is included by Jesus in a list of sins that defile a man.

- John 1:47 Jesus considered the fact that Nathaniel was a man without deceit to be worthy of specific mention.

- 1 Peter 2:1 Peter instructs us to rid ourselves of all deceit.

- 1 Peter 2:22 Speaking of the Lord, Peter mentions His having no sin and being without deceit in the same breath.

- Revelation 14:5 A select group who are highly commended in Heaven are described as having no fault and without deceit.

It is apparent then, that God places a high value on our not being deceitful. This should not be surprising because God Himself is righteous in all His works. Balaam said that "God is not a man that He should lie" (Numbers 23:19). In other words, God is different from us in that He is incapable of being dishonest. If we want to grow closer to Him, we have to become more like Him and deceitfulness cannot be part of our lives.

There is a sobering passage of Scripture, found in 2 Samuel 22:27. God says that He will show Himself pure to those who are pure but to those who are devious He will behave very differently. If we commit ourselves to a lifestyle of deceit, He will allow us to suffer the consequences and we ourselves will be deceived. There is a similar thought in Revelation 22:11. What this passage is saying is that we will become more of what we are. If we are righteous, we will become more righteous, but if we are unrighteous we will become more unrighteous. God gives considerable latitude to us to choose our own pathway, and although in His compassion He will try to correct us if we are on the wrong path, there comes a time when He will respect our decision and allow us to continue. Examples of this are King Saul and Judas Iscariot, both of whom had been chosen for high positions, but in the end lost everything. We should take note that both of them were dishonest men.

If we are to grow in God we have to have a love for the truth; the truth in His Word and the truth in our interactions with others. It cannot be superficial but stem from an honest love for truth from our heart, regardless of how it might require changes to our life. We have to seek the Lord to "Create in me a clean heart" (Ps 51:10), one that does not have elements of mixture, and we will find that God does indeed reward those who value the truth.

Further discussion:
- Compare the end result of Bible characters who sinned and confessed their faults to those who continued in their sin.
- Discuss the passages in the chapter and other passages that describe God's position regarding deceitfulness.
- Consider passages in the Bible that describe how God will respond to those who are liars and deceitful people.

CHAPTER SEVEN

Prayer and Bible Study

We have heard so many times that prayer and Bible study are essentials to our Christian walk. This is true. Prayer and Bible study bring life to us and are indispensable to Christian growth. However, sometimes they become a burden because they are regarded as tasks that must be performed whereas really they are a wonderful enrichment to our lives. There have been many books written on the subjects of prayer and Bible study by men and women who are very knowledgeable and have wonderful teaching to share, so here we will only look at a few things that have been helpful to me.

PRAYER

I recall as a young Christian being quite overwhelmed regarding prayer. I had heard stories of men and women who spent hours alone with God, praying and interceding, but my own concentration span was limited to a few minutes. It was very discouraging. As time went on, I found that although I still struggled with periods of time in prayer, I talked with the Lord spontaneously throughout the day. I shared my life with Him, talking about things that happened, hopes, fears, my family, my work, the state of the county… all manner of subjects. Prayer had become more like conversation with a friend.

One day I read a quotation from A. W. Tozer that helped me greatly. Tozer said that he seldom prayed for more than twenty-five minutes, but that he seldom went more than twenty-five minutes without praying. This sounded more like something that I could do and if that was Tozer's prayer life, I didn't need to feel that I was failing if I could not maintain my concentration for long periods. The apostle Paul instructed the Thessalonian church to "Pray without ceasing," (1 Thessalonians 5:17) and it would seem that this is just how Tozer lived. I do not want in any way to diminish the importance and impact upon events, even world events, of those who do spend long periods of time in prayer and intercession. Their contribution is enormous and I aspire to be like them. But a life of communication that Tozer experienced speaks of constant fellowship with God through the day and it was a great encouragement to me, coming from a man of his stature.

It never ceases to amaze me that God has the slightest interest in me and other people, when He is so great and we are so not. It is not as if we are models of perfection like Him, but rather we are like sheep who require much patience to lead and who tend to wander, making poor choices and having to constantly be guided into the right places. God indeed is very merciful toward us. The truth is though, that He does take an interest in even small things in our lives. Some years ago, I was trying to resolve a problem at my place of work. I had been trying unsuccessfully for three days and eventually I stopped and asked the Lord for His help. Almost immediately, I knew what to do and the problem was solved in twenty minutes. Twenty minutes!! You might well wonder why I did not ask for help sooner and obviously I should have done so, but

I think that God wanted to teach me something about His interest and care over all matters of life. A problem that had defeated me for three days took no time to resolve when He showed me the answer.

Just as I believe Tozer found, prayer involves an aspect of earnestly seeking God to move in a given situation and also an aspect of fellowship. A passage of the Bible that is important for us with regards to our prayer relationship with God is found in Psalm 65:4 where we read, "Blessed is the man You choose, and cause to approach You, that he may dwell in Your courts." Let's consider some thoughts from these words.

First of all, someone that God will invite into His presence is blessed. That is a gross understatement. The very nature of God is such that being anywhere close to Him is a wonderful experience indeed. We see this in the book of Revelation where in chapters four and five, we have a description of the worship and exultation of God that takes place around His throne. He is so majestic, so awe-inspiring, so indescribable, that it is impossible not to reverence and worship Him.

It is a wonderful thing for us to experience His presence here on earth. Sometimes the Lord comes with great joy, sometimes with great peace. Sometimes, His presence is known by a sweet fragrance of spices that one can smell. Sometimes He comes with an awesome sense of holiness that leaves us speechless, riveted, even for long periods of time while His presence remains. Sometimes he comes as a friend, as if He just wants to share the time with us. But however He comes, He is always full of goodness and we are always uplifted. To use the word of the psalm, we are blessed.

Secondly, we see that it is God's prerogative as to who He chooses to approach Him. It is not something for us to attain by our hard work or to qualify ourselves by our exploits for God. So why would God select one person over another? This is a question that could be asked many times over in the Bible as we look at the different people whom He chose. For instance, why did Jesus select the men who became His disciples, the foundation of the church? In the early days, they seemed to struggle to understand what He was saying and had trouble "getting it." Peter clearly was not a stable man, prone to rash decisions, and hardly suitable to lead a great work. But Jesus knew what Peter would become. As always, God looks at the heart, not outward appearances. So, we need to humbly ask the Lord to work in our heart to change us so that we might become people that He would choose for this high privilege of approaching Him.

Thirdly, the psalm presents the opportunity to not just visit His courts but for them to be a place where we can dwell, or remain. We can go through life knowing His wonderful presence on a normal basis. It is mind-blowing to think that God would offer such a privilege and experience to us.

BIBLE STUDY

The importance of Bible reading and Bible study cannot be overstated. The Bible is truly an amazing book, having been written over a period of about 1,500 years by a total of forty different people. These people came from widely divergent backgrounds… kings, shepherds, tradesmen, professionals, the educated and the uneducated. They wrote about different things pertaining to different time periods, yet amazingly, their writings are harmonious. Their portrayal of the nature of God and of man agrees. If we were to take forty men and women from a cross-section of society and ask them to write about a particular subject, any subject, it is highly unlikely that they would all be in agreement, regardless of whatever subject was selected. They would have differing political standpoints, moral standpoints, religious standpoints, opinions on priorities in life, and of almost everything else. So to have a group of forty people writing harmoniously over a period of 1,500 years is no small achievement. It could only come about though a single person overseeing the writing, and of course, that person can only be God.

Another aspect of the Bible that sets it apart from all other writings is the element of prophecy. No book contains prophecies like the Bible, so many of which have been fulfilled already. Many of the prophecies were given hundreds of years in advance of the event, and many of them are very detailed. For example, the return of the Jews to the land of Israel that took place in the middle of the last century was prophesied by Jeremiah more than four hundred years before the birth of Christ. The Jews were not regathered to Israel until about 1,900 years after the sacking of Jerusalem by the Romans in AD70 which had led to their being dispersed through much of the world. However, Jeremiah prophesied this return even before the first sacking of Jerusalem by the Babylonians and the subsequent deportation of the Jews to Babylon!

Some of the Bible prophecies even have time periods for their fulfillment. One of these was the period that the Jews would be in Babylon (seventy years) before being restored to their land (Jeremiah 29:10). An examination of the incredible volume, detail, and accuracy of Bible prophecy can only lead one to the conclusion, that God inspired the Book.

In spite of the evidence to support the Divine inspiration of the Bible, we still have to accept by faith the things that are written because we cannot prove that it is inspired. Or can we? There was a Russian mathematician who lived from 1855 to 1942 named Ivan Panin. He immigrated to the United States, was educated at Harvard, and was such a highly regarded speaker that he could command "top dollar" fees for the lectures that he conducted on Russian literature.

The original languages in which the Bible was written, mostly Hebrew and Greek, do not have numbers but use alphabet characters to represent numbers. One day, Panin was reading Genesis 1:1 and being a mathematician, he noticed numeric patterns of the words which intrigued him. Panin was an agnostic but he became a Christian after exploring the numeric patterns and becoming convinced of the inspiration of the Bible. Panin devoted fifty years of his life to mathematically proving the Bible, compiling 40,000 pages of detailed handwritten notes in the process.

Panin researched sections of the Bible until he was satisfied that each section was inspired. His findings showed that the laws of probability ran into the billions or more against the likelihood of the Bible being written by man. We have no trouble believing in DNA as conclusive proof of a person's identity and it is used to convict and acquit people suspected of crimes. Really, if we believe in the unerring accuracy of DNA, we ought also to believe in the unerring accuracy of the Bible, based on the same laws of probability.

Panin ran advertisements in newspapers, challenging anyone to disprove his findings, and the few that tried had only lame suppositions. He also challenged a group of Harvard professors to develop a sentence in English on any subject that matched the mathematical patterns of the Bible. Genesis 1:1 has thirty patterns of the number seven and the professors could not come close to thirty. They had a significant advantage too, because using the English language meant that they had about 400,000 words available to them compared to 4,500 Hebrew words that would have been available to the writer of Genesis. Panin and other scholars also re-examined other works of Hebrew literature to see if they could find similar mathematical patterns but found that they were only in the Bible. Essentially, Panin mathematically proved the Bible to be inspired. (Refer to *The Inspiration of Scriptures Scientifically Demonstrated* by Ivan Panin).

There have been people who criticized Panin's work but none could actually refute it. It is possible that one day, with the aid of modern computers, someone will develop a sentence or more with the same patterns that are in the Bible. However, should someone be successful it will only reinforce the fact that the Bible had to be inspired, because those forty writers did not have computers. Moreover, will someone be able to write an entire book with over 783,000 words? If the feat should ever be accomplished, it will only help to prove the Divine inspiration of the Bible because the mind of man could not accomplish the feat alone.

There is simply no substitute in the Christian life for reading the Bible. It is good to listen to sermons, read books, and utilize other helps to improve our knowledge and understanding, but our own personal reading is by far the most important means. Often when we read a section we find that we have quickly forgotten what we just read but the sense of those words remains with us. The Bible provides us with clear instruction for life and it is immensely practical and full of wisdom. By reading the Bible, over time we grow in our knowledge of God and how He thinks, thereby developing the spiritual aspects of our life too. There is no other book like it.

Further discussion:
- If prayer has been difficult, teach yourself to regard it as conversing with God and something that takes place naturally. Consider it a delight. I am confident that God will make Himself known to you in a greater degree.
- Read Revelation chapters four and five and consider carefully the awesome worship of God that takes place

around His throne. Ask the Lord to develop the same spirit of worship in your own life.
- As you read your Bible, record passages where God describes Himself. These will help you to understand His nature and what is important to Him.

CHAPTER EIGHT

The Use of our Time

Time is something that is limited. Each day has twenty-four hours, no more and no less, and we cannot change that. We do not have control over time itself but we do have control over how we use it. For example, if two people have a commute to work that takes an hour, one person might decide that the time could be better spent doing something else and seek employment closer to home, or perhaps move from their current residence to live closer to work. The other person might decide to listen to messages or Bible readings because the time in the car allows an opportunity alone that would not otherwise be available. In this illustration, both people find a way to make better use of their time, although each has a different solution. The important aspect is not what remedial action they took but that they did take action to avoid wasting the time.

Let us consider two parables. In Matthew 25:14-30 we have the parable of the talents. A man was about to travel and he gave talents to his servants. To one he gave five talents, to another he gave two talents, and to a third he gave one talent. The first two servants invested their money and doubled what they had been given. The third hid his talent in the ground. When the master returned, he commended the first two servants. Although they had been given different amounts, they both received the same commendation ("well done, good and faithful servant") and because of their faithfulness in small things they would both be made rulers over many things. The master's response to the third servant was entirely different. That servant was called lazy and rebuked for not having at least gained interest on the money. The master took his talent from him and cast him into "outer darkness" which we believe to be a place in hell.

We can compare this parable with a similar one in Luke 19:11-27. Again, there were servants who were given money by their master, but in this case each was given the same amount, a mina. The first servant earned ten more minas and was given rule over ten cities. Similarly, the second servant earned five minas and was rewarded with five cities. But one servant, like the third servant in the parable of the talents, kept his mina and returned it without any gain and was described as a "wicked servant" and condemned for not having at least earned interest.

In the parable of the talents, the servants were given differing amounts, but in the parable of the minas the servants were given the same amount. The first parable recognizes that we have different levels of ability and we are expected to make the most of those abilities. The servant with the five talents did not have the same abilities as the one with ten, but both received the same commendation and reward because both had made the most of what they had. However, in the parable of the minas, all servants began with the same amount and their rewards varied depending on what they had produced.

We should ask ourselves, what would be comparable to a mina in our life, something that we all have in common and at the same level? One such thing is time. We all have the same amount of time available to us. Based on the parable, how we use that time will determine the degree of reward.

There are many things that demand our time and most of these are good things that we should be including into our day or week. They include our work, time for our spouse, time for our family, social time, Bible reading and Bible study, prayer, church attendance, ministry and serving, relaxation, exercise, eating, sleeping, and others. Obviously, we want to allocate our time between the various demands so that everything is covered adequately and in proper balance.

Maintaining a balance in our lives is not easy. Life has competing demands for our time and it also has its surprises which can unexpectedly force us to make changes in our time allocation. These may be brief changes or they may last for a season. For example, some years ago I accepted a job offer in a different city from the one in which I was living. The company wanted me to start in March but my wife and I did not want to move the family until after the school year finished in June. For the ensuing three months, the normal allocation of my time was significantly changed because I was in one city and my wife and family were in another and our time together was limited to periodic weekend visits. We could adjust our routine to keep in touch through phone calls but obviously other aspects of life changed. Our social time was eliminated. I spent more time than usual at work because being alone, I could devote the time to learning the new job without impacting the family. Church attendance was unaffected for my wife and family, but for me it was severely disrupted and my involvement in some aspect of serving became non-existent. However, soon after we relocated the family, we began to re-establish our normal allocation of time because that season of separation was over.

Being successful in managing our time requires two important ingredients; discipline and planning. If we are not disciplined, we will never allocate our time well and in fact, a lack of self-discipline has a negative effect on most aspects of our life, perhaps even all aspects. Further, if we do not plan our time, we will not accomplish all the things that are important to us. It is easy to delay the start of something or to spend more time on it than is necessary. Both discipline and planning are essential to accomplishments.

Successful people have always been disciplined people and this included Jesus. We can see self-discipline in many occasions of His life. One such example is the episode in the wilderness when Jesus was tempted by the devil. In Matthew 4:1-4 we read the account of how He had been fasting for forty days and His hunger had returned. The devil suggested that He turn some of the stones into bread to alleviate His hunger. Jesus was later to turn water into wine, restore sight to the blind, walk on water, and heal all manner of diseases, so making bread from stones was not going to challenge His divine capabilities. No one was present, so it would have been easy to succumb to the temptation. After all, He needed to eat soon anyway so what would be the problem with complying with the devil's suggestion?

Although seemingly innocent, this suggestion was not the direction of the Father. It was a temptation from the devil, and Jesus wasn't about to give in no matter how hungry He felt. He took His instructions from the Father, not from the devil. It must have required considerable self-discipline to resist the temptation and wait a little longer for His food but being disciplined was an essential quality for the fulfilment of His purpose on Earth. We see discipline in many of the recorded events of His life, and Jesus did indeed fulfill His purpose. Without being disciplined, He would never have made it to the cross and the plan of salvation would have failed.

Being disciplined in the use of our time is so important. Sometimes we fall into a habit of staying up late at night, which results in an inadequate amount of sleep and tiredness during the day. This may mean that we are less productive in the things that are more important to us.

Another important aspect of being disciplined is to finish what we start. One of my teenage grandsons was helping with a weekend construction project for a small church. When the project was completed, the other workers began to leave and he stopped them by saying, "The job is not finished until the tools have been put away." He was right. All those tools could not be left because they were on loan from other individuals and they needed to be returned. The tools were not going to be stowed in the back of the truck by themselves. We have to be people who have the discipline to pay attention to details and finish what we start. Successful people pay attention to details and have the discipline to carry them through.

Just as we see discipline in the life of Jesus, we also see planning. When word came to Him that Lazarus was sick, He delayed setting out for Bethany for two days. His intent was to raise Lazarus from the dead and teach on His being "The Resurrection and the Life" and He wanted there to be no question that raising Lazarus would be a miracle. Had Jesus left immediately, Lazarus would have been dead but probably the degree of decay of his body would not have been such that it produced an odor when the stone that sealed the entrance to the tomb was moved away. This would have left open the opportunity for a skeptic to say that Lazarus had actually hidden in the tomb until Jesus arrived to create the impression of being raised from the dead. By planning the time of His departure and knowing how long the journey would take, Jesus arrived when Lazarus had been dead for four days. In so doing, He left no doubt that when He raised Lazarus from the dead it was an astonishing and undeniable miracle.

A technique that I have found helpful in planning is to think backward. If I have to be at a certain place at a certain time and I have to buy a present and gas on the way, I will consider how much time each of these pieces will take and by combining the time for each piece, I can estimate when I need to leave the house in order to arrive at the destination on time. It is a technique used in manufacturing businesses too, where sophisticated ERP (Enterprise Resource Planning) systems establish when production of a part needs to commence to meet the required delivery date to the customer. The system calculates the start date by considering the contracted delivery date, lead times for ordering and receiving the raw materials from suppliers, and the lead time for manufacturing the various sub-assemblies that will be assembled into the final product. Essentially, the system knows the necessary time for each step and works backward from the required delivery date to calculate the start date.

When we consider the proper use of our time, we tend to think of how to be productive, just as we have been discussing discipline and planning in the preceding paragraphs. However, an important consideration is also rest. One of the Ten Commandments is to honor the Sabbath Day. The principle behind this commandment is to rest every seventh day, which we do to honor God and also for our own benefit. God who made us, knows that we need rest and we honor Him by setting aside a day to put Him first, such as by attending a local church, and by resting to refresh ourselves. We need to be refreshed both physically and mentally.

Sometimes we fritter away time on unimportant things, and we can't get that time back. Also, what might be an acceptable use of time for one person may not be so for another. We must be open to the Lord's instruction for us in this matter. There are plenty of things available to waste our time, although none of them may be wrong in themselves or at least not in some measure. Making proper, balanced use of our time is not easy but it is important. Perhaps it is like a mina that the Lord has given to us to invest wisely.

Further discussion:
- Write down how your time is allocated in a typical week. Evaluate this allocation to see if there should be adjustments. In particular, look for things that are not productive that could be replaced by more productive things.
- Consider the life of Jesus and discuss additional instances that show discipline in His life.
- Consider your "Sabbath" day, which for most of us is Sunday. What do you do to honor God on this day? What do you do to rest and refresh your body and mind? In what ways is this day different from the other days of the week?

CHAPTER NINE

Expanding by Contracting

A walk with God has its apparent dichotomies and seemingly contradictory aspects. One of these is how growth comes from living within boundaries. Our natural thinking tells us that growth is expanding our present boundaries, not diminishing them. It is reaching into new areas, developing new spiritual skills, and enlarging our understanding and experience of God. All of this is very true and we will not grow without extending our boundaries. However, our spiritual growth is also in no small part, dependent upon our willingness to allow our lives to be restricted in certain areas. Sometimes this is removing a behavior that we have come to realize is sinful, disobedient, or in some way displeasing to Him. That really should be obvious. However, there will be other things that God requires of us for our own good, and our obedience or disobedience will determine the degree of anointing that will be upon our life and ministry. Regardless of what the issue may be, certain areas of our life have to become limited in order for the important spiritual areas to grow.

An example of this is found in the instructions to priests and in particular to the high priest in the Old Testament Law. In Leviticus 21 we find some specific commands to them from the Lord. One of these related to who a man could marry. Men in the general public had considerable latitude as to who they could choose for a wife but there were restrictions placed on priests. They could not marry someone who had been a prostitute or a divorcee. When it came to the high priest, the requirements were even more restrictive. In addition to the requirements for priests, the wife of the high priest had to be an Israelite and a virgin, not even a widow.

Another requirement for priests and the high priest related to the burial of the dead. The general public had no limitations, other than after having buried a dead person they would be considered unclean for seven days. Priests however, were not allowed to bury dead people except for immediate family such as parents and children. The restriction for the high priest was greater still and, in fact, he was not permitted to have anything to do with a dead person regardless of how close the relationship might be. No doubt this would have been a considerable sacrifice when a loved one such as a parent died, but that was the limitation that God placed on him because of his office as high priest. So we see that God placed more stringent requirements on priests, and even more still on the high priest, than on the general public.

We might question why God required these limitations. Were they not men, just like the men of the general public? Really, what difference would it make if they participated in burials…would that not show compassion for people and especially for loved ones? The answer is simply that these restrictions were required by God. Keeping them showed two important things; (1) the man was obedient to God, and (2) he loved God above others, even close relatives. Pleasing Him was the most important thing.

What benefit was it to a priest to be obedient to God in these matters? The benefit was considerable indeed. When we look at the tabernacle of Moses we find that the general public was only permitted into the Outer Court. This contained the altar of sacrifice and the laver which would speak to us of our salvation and water baptism, foundational issues in our Christian walk. The Outer Court was an area that was uncovered and therefore had limited protection. Also, the source of light was natural light, that of the sun or moon. Priests, however, were permitted into the Holy Place where there was a greater revelation of God. That section was covered, providing shelter and protection, and the source of light was the candlestick, speaking of the seven spirits of God which are mentioned several times in the book of Revelation and specifically identified in Isaiah chapter eleven. Spiritually, it represented a significant advancement over the experiences and revelation of God that was available in the Outer Court.

Finally, the high priest enjoyed the greatest privilege of all by being permitted into the Holy of Holies where the Ark of the Covenant and the Mercy Seat were located. As with the Holy Place, there was shelter and protection and a further advancement in experiences and revelation. There the source of light was the very glory of the presence of God. It was the place where God chose to dwell and to speak from. It was such a sacred place that although the high priest was allowed to enter, he could do so only on one occasion of the year, on the Day of Atonement. It was the highest privilege available to the entire nation, to be able to be in the place where God had chosen to dwell amongst His people.

So we see from this chapter in Leviticus that the restrictions placed upon priests and the high priest qualified them for significantly greater blessings than were available to the general public. They were granted a greater revelation of God and a closer proximity to His presence. In the same manner, God may place certain limitations upon us and our obedience to them will qualify us for greater blessings too. God wants us to run our race without weights which handicap us and slow us down (Hebrews 12:1). Weights are probably not sin in a general sense of behavior but, if there is some restriction that God places on us, it becomes sin to us if we are disobedient. These things which we identify as weights may be perfectly in order for many other Christians, but if we are to grow in our relationship with God and in the effectiveness of our ministry they are not in order for us. We must be willing to run our race without being handicapped and this will mean that to reach higher planes we may not have all the freedoms that are permitted to others.

There are many examples in the Bible, one being John the Baptist. His life was decidedly unusual. Firstly, his clothing was made of camel's hair. This provided excellent insulation from the cold, necessary for his outdoor living, and the undercoat of the hair was soft so that the garment was comfortable. However, to say the least, John's wardrobe was very limited and not reflective of an important person. It was reminiscent of the children of Israel's journey through the wilderness where they wore the same clothing that they brought out of Egypt as slaves for forty years because it did not wear out. John's diet was also limited, one of honey and locusts. This does not sound particularly interesting, and perhaps like the children of Israel he would have liked some quail occasionally. One might wonder why John could not have expanded his wardrobe and diet, but this was the life that God had called him to walk.

So what kind of man was John in the eyes of God? Well, Jesus said that there was no one greater among men (Matthew 11:11). When most of the people of his day, including the religious leaders, failed to recognize Jesus as the Christ, John was the one who introduced Him as such. Moreover, John understood the mission of Jesus when others, including the disciples of Jesus, did not. John described him as "The Lamb of God who takes away the sin of the world." John made this pronouncement even before Jesus had spoken a word of teaching or performed a single miracle. Like the populace, the disciples were looking for a Christ who would deliver the nation from the domination of the Romans, but John understood that He would be like a sacrificial lamb, an offering for the cleansing of sin. John may have given up many things that were reasonable expectations in a person's life, but he was rewarded with the revelation of Jesus being the Christ and perhaps even more astoundingly, the revelation of the primary ministry of Jesus. John had restrictions in his life but his ministry expanded mightily as a result of his obedience to the will of God for him.

I have observed that those who grow into a closer walk with God and possess a clearer understanding of Him have certain things that are important "habits" in their lives and other things that they simply will not do. Frequently, these things are seemingly insignificant and violating them would not be considered sin by any stretch of the imagination. Also, they are not necessarily the common practice amongst other good and upright Christians. However, God has directed these individuals with regard to these particular things and their obedience to God demonstrates their desire to put Him first no matter how trivial His wishes may appear. It is not a legalistic adherence to a set of rules, nor is it an attempt to attain to spiritual maturity through good works or pious self-denial. Rather, it is obedience to God, even in seemingly small matters, and it stems from a heart that simply loves Him. God has His reasons for the things that He requires of us and they are always for our ultimate benefit.

The restrictions that God places in our life were likened by Jesus to a vine being pruned (John Chapter 15). If we consider this illustration, unproductive branches are cut away from the vine so that the flow of sap is not wasted on those branches. The result is that the vine produces more fruit that it would otherwise have been able. God applies the same principle to our lives, removing things that are not productive. As already noted, these things may not be sin but we will not advance to higher planes with the excess baggage.

Most of us do not like to hear about being pruned. There is a tendency to focus on what we are giving up. This is contrary to the truth of Scripture, for in Hebrews we read that the result of being disciplined is the "peaceable fruit of righteousness" (Hebrews 12:11). To know peace in our lives is a wonderful, wonderful blessing. It is something that is sought after through relationships, through financial security, and the satisfaction of accomplishments. However, peace is elusive because it is not attained through any of these means. Peace is a product of righteousness, and in fact we cannot experience peace without righteousness. When the Father prunes us of unproductive branches, our obedience is considered righteousness and the peace that we experience becomes greater. This can be both peace within ourselves and a peace that surrounds our life. We should focus on what we are gaining by being pruned, not on what we are losing, because the joy and blessing of the increased fruitfulness far outweighs the cost.

A word of warning... if God should place some restrictions upon us we should never consider ourselves better or more spiritual than others who do not have those same restrictions. We are not better than them but rather, God is working in our life for a different purpose. Similarly, we should not look for things to give up, thinking that by so doing we will win favor with God and become more spiritual. It has to be God's direction in order to bear fruit. Just as our salvation is not attained by works, by the things that we can do to earn it, so too is the case with our spiritual growth.

We will not grow simply because we decide to restrict ourselves in some manner. Spiritual growth comes through obedience. If we were to limit our wardrobe and eat a very restricted diet, would that make us a mighty man of God like John the Baptist? I really doubt it. More likely, we would become "super-spiritual," self-righteous, and probably miserable. But when we are obedient to God in a matter, even a seemingly trivial matter, He rewards us. It is not that we do something for the prospect of reward... the motive is our love for the Lord and desire to please and honor Him. However, we do find that He truly is a "rewarder of those who diligently seek Him" (Hebrews 11:6).

Further discussion:
- Consider a situation in your life where God has pruned an unproductive aspect. What subsequent blessings did you receive within the following year?
- What things might be considered "weights" in our lives, things that are not sin but nevertheless can impede our spiritual walk?
- Samson and Samuel were both men who were appointed by God and both were instructed to live with restrictions (Judges 13:5, 1 Samuel 1:11). Consider how obedient they were to God in this matter, the length and productiveness of their ministry, and their ultimate end.

Crossing Over to a Closer Walk with God

CHAPTER TEN

The Example of the Apostle John

There have been many saints with a close walk with the Lord, but during Jesus' time on earth, there was no one closer to Him than the Apostle John. Therefore it should be helpful to us to examine the gospel record of John and his writings to learn about him and what he considered important. Let us first consider some events that demonstrate the closeness of friendship between Jesus and John.

- In his gospel, John refers to himself as the disciple "whom Jesus loved" on three occasions (John 20:2, 21:7, 21:20). This indicates a degree of affinity that surpassed the other disciples.

- On the cross, when Jesus saw fit to place his mother in the care of a trusted friend, He chose John (John 19:26). It is surprising that He did not leave the care of his mother to His half-brothers, James and Jude, who would soon become apostles themselves. James actually became the head of the Jerusalem church so it is not as if these men were unreliable or of questionable character. It speaks volumes that Jesus requested John to be the one to care for his mother, even over His good brothers.

- At the Last Supper, it was John who sat to the right of Jesus, leaning upon Him. Jesus is now seated at the right hand of the Father, the right side being the place of pre-eminence, so being at the right side of Jesus on this history-making occasion would have been a privileged position.

- Also at the Last Supper, when Jesus announced that one of the Twelve would betray Him, Peter motioned to John to ask Jesus who it would be. Peter must have known that if Jesus would divulge this information to anyone it would be John. Had he not been so confident that Jesus would tell John, Peter would have found a way to ask the question himself, even though he must not have been conveniently seated near Jesus. Peter was not known for being bashful.

- Jesus did indeed tell John the identity of the betrayer. This revealed an enormous degree of trust because John could then have conveyed that information to the others and even prevented Judas from leaving. I'm sure Peter would have happily used his sword on Judas or some other means had John cried out to stop him from leaving the room. John could have ruined the whole plan of salvation, or at least postponed it for a year (because Jesus had to die at the Feast of Passover), but Jesus knew His friend and knew that the secret would be safe.

- Another evidence of the closeness of the relationship between Jesus and John is the degree of revelation that was given to John. The New Testament writers, particularly the writers of the letters, were given considerable insight into the mysteries of God and of future events, but none more so than John. We talk about the deepest matters in our hearts with those who are closest to us and it would seem that the same is true of Jesus. John was granted the incredible visions of future events that were recorded by him in the Book of Revelation. To him was given extensive understanding of the Last Days, even events beyond the Second Coming of Christ. Other saints such as Paul were also granted considerable insight but it is fair to say that John's was unique.

Now let us consider what John considered to be important in the Christian walk.

(a) Love for the Lord. When one reads the opening verses of John's first letter (1 John 1:1-4), one is struck by the sense of love in his heart for the Lord. And when he says that he is writing to pass on things that will make the joy of the readers full, one knows that John himself must have been full of joy. John truly loved the Lord...no wonder that he was full of joy.

(b) Christian growth. John was concerned that the people who were under his leadership continue to grow in their Christian walk.

He likened spiritual growth to natural growth by categorizing Christians into one of three groups… children, young men, and fathers (1 John 2:12-14). We examined this in another chapter so we will not make further comment, other than the observation that growth was important to John.

(c) Love for others. John had a deep love for the Lord but he also had a deep love for people. Throughout his letter are references to the importance of having love. Some of the passages are as follows:

- 1 John 4:11 "Beloved, if God so loved us, we ought to love one another."

- 1 John 3:18 "…Let us not love in word or in tongue, but in deed and in truth."

- 1 John 4:20 "If someone says, "I love God," and hates his brother, he is a liar…."

One cannot read his letter without being impressed by the importance that he attached to having love in our lives. His writing on the subject is very pointed, leaving no room for anything short of being perfect in love.

(d) Righteousness. John was a righteous man himself and he exhorted his readers to live righteous lives too. John was very clear in his assessment of those who claimed to live righteously.

- He expected Christians to overcome sin. 1 John 5:18 "…whoever is born of God does not commit sin…" John does not mean that we never sin but that we do not maintain sinful patterns and accommodate the continual practice of a sin in our life.

- He allowed no place for failure to keep the commands of God. 1 John 2:4 "He who says 'I know Him' and does not keep His commandments, is a liar, and the truth is not in him."

(e) Fellowship with the Father and the Son. Fellowship was not just important to John, it was an integral part of his life. He truly walked with the Lord and fellowship with Him was something that he experienced and understood. Therefore, John was able to pass on to us how to have fellowship with God. In 1 John 1:7 he wrote, "But if we walk in the light as He is in the light we have fellowship one with another…" Fellowship is defined as "an association of persons with similar tastes, a friendly relationship, companionship." It is astonishing that we can have fellowship with God by this definition because He is so much greater than us. True fellowship was unquestionably John's experience and he wanted his readers to experience it too.

Let us consider this thought of fellowship with God further because it is really the whole point of the Christian walk. John said that we must walk in the light just as God is in the light, and in encouraging us to step up, he implies that not everyone has that fellowship with God. Therefore we need to ask ourselves, what does it mean to walk in the light? Light is something that dispels darkness. We may have difficulty seeing objects when it is dark but not so in the light of day. Therefore walking in the light is to be entirely visible in a spiritual sense. It means that our heart and motives are pure, without guile. We are to be consistent, not better behaved when we are being watched, not projecting an image at church and then conducting ourselves differently at home and at work.

As we address issues and bring our life into conformity with the Lord's commands, we grow in fellowship with Him. The starting point for change is our having the desire to do so. The agents for change are our will and the Holy Spirit. We can liken it to walking, where we have two legs to propel ourselves forward. One leg represents the things that we must do and the other represents the things that only God can do. Our part is to align ourselves with Him and seek to do what is right, but we need Him to actually enable us to be changed. It is like the passage in Romans 12:1-2 where Paul instructs us to be transformed. By using the passive tense, he makes clear that our part is to allow ourselves to be transformed, but the actual transforming is accomplished by another, namely the Holy Spirit, through the renewing of our mind.

John was the gospel writer who recorded Jesus' promise to reveal Himself to those who are His friends, who love Him and keep His commandments (John 14:21), and I believe John wrote from his own experience of this in his letter. To reveal something is to make known what was previously concealed. There are many aspects of our Christian life that must be taken by faith because God cannot be seen. We see evidence of Him, but because He is not actually visible we must accept these things by faith. However, Jesus said that he would reveal Himself to those who love Him and keep His commandments, so there is a high degree of fellowship with Him that is possible for us to enjoy. It is a relationship reserved for friends and companions.

In what way does Jesus reveal Himself? Did He mean this in a spiritual sense or a literal sense where a person actually sees Him from time-to-time? I cannot say that I know the answer; certainly the former, but perhaps both could be true. However, we can surely say that as our walk with Him grows closer, as there is a refining and greater degree of obedience in us, our understanding of His ways grows and our experience of His presence is more wonderful. The better we know Him, the more we love Him. There is a sense of adoration that is resident within us, just like we sense about the Apostle John as he writes about the Lord.

Further discussion:
- In this chapter, we looked at aspects of John's life that demonstrated the closeness of His relationship with the Lord. What would an observer point to in your life that demonstrates your own relationship with Him?
- Often a weakness in our life becomes a strength after the Lord has dealt with it. John initially wanted to call down the fire of judgement on people but became a man full of love. Can you think of others in the Bible whose weakness became a strength?
- Consider the definition of fellowship... "An association of persons with similar tastes, a friendly relationship, companionship." How does this translate into the kind of person with whom God desires to have fellowship?

CHAPTER ELEVEN

The Keys

In his letter to the Philippian Christians, the apostle Paul writes about the Lord Jesus and how He left Heaven to come to Earth as a man (Philippians 2:5-8). It is astonishing to think that Jesus would give up so much in order to become the means for our reconciliation to God. It truly shows the extent of His love for us. He had been in the form, or appearance, of God but took on a body to become a man, a "species" that He had created. What an amazing display of love, for the creator to take the appearance of the created, to accept man's significant limitations and to live in his domain. We don't know what the "form of God" is like, nor do we know just how becoming a man would have affected the Lord, but we can certainly understand that coming to Earth to live like we do was no small change!

Having become man, Jesus had to live like man. In terms of natural things, this entailed requiring food, sleep, and the other basics that we need each day. However, the purpose of the life of Jesus was not just to live like man but at the same time to accomplish the will of the Father, and to this end He had to retain the same perfect relationship that He had known in Heaven. In the gospels, we read about this relationship in terms such as, "the Son does...what He sees the Father do" (John 5:19), and "I do not seek My own will but the will of the Father who sent Me" (John 5:30), and "he who has seen Me has seen the Father" (John 14:9). These verses show us that Jesus and the Father were very close indeed!

Now that Jesus was a man, certain things would become essential to preserving His relationship with the Father. Paul identifies these as the qualities of humility and obedience. To quote Paul, Jesus came "...in the likeness of men. And being found in appearance as a man, He humbled Himself and became obedient to the point of death, even the death of the cross" (Philippians 2:7-8). We could say that in Heaven, the relationship between the Father and the Son was one of perfect communication and understanding, completely unhindered because they were on an equal footing. However, when Jesus lived on Earth as a man, He potentially faced hinderances to this communication because now He was Man as well as God. The means for Jesus to overcome these hinderances was to possess the qualities of humility and obedience. His humility and obedience were the keys to His continued relationship with the Father. We can also say that if these qualities were essential for Jesus, they must also be essential for us, people who live in a body on the Earth. If a person wants to excel in something such as a sport, they train hard. If a person wants to come close to God, they are humble and obedient. It is what they do.

Humility and obedience do not come easily to us. We are far more prone to exhibit the opposite qualities of pride and disobedience. A humble person is someone with a modest estimate of their own importance, someone who recognizes that all he or she has was given by God. An obedient person lives by the teachings of the Bible, not trying to make it fit their own wishes but wholeheartedly seeking to live in a manner that is pleasing to God.

In addition, we must also be obedient to the specific instructions that God gives to us, which may be as simple as sharing a word of encouragement with someone. Often it is the small things that we disregard or overlook but all are important for us.

The end of the lives of people who were humble and obedient compared to those who were prideful and disobedient is very different,, and there are many examples of both in the Bible. Let us consider two individuals, Moses and Elijah, who had extraordinary achievements but were humble and obedient. Moses exhibited such humility that he was described as being more humble than "all men who were on the face of the earth" (Numbers 12:3). His obedience in leading the Israelites through the wilderness to the Promised Land was complete in even the smallest detail, other than the one occasion when he struck the rock twice instead of speaking to it. Similarly, Elijah was obedient to the instructions of God in proclaiming a drought, even though he must have known it would result in hardship for himself and that his life would be in jeopardy. And although Elijah saw God work in astonishing power through him, he displayed a humble attitude, never taking credit to himself.

The relationship that Moses and Elijah developed with God was evident upon the Mount of Transfiguration (Matthew 17:1-8). Here Jesus was seen shining with the brilliance of the glory of God, and talking to none other than Moses and Elijah. We might have thought He would be talking to Gabriel and Michael, the two archangels, but instead it was two men. Men who had become His close friends.

Let us summarize the points from Paul's letter to the Philippians as follows:

- In Heaven, Jesus was in the form of God. That was His appearance before coming to Earth. He was like the Father.

- Jesus was not inferior to the Father but was equal to Him.

- He became a man, living like us on the Earth.

- Having become a man, there were two characteristics that were essential in order to maintain His relationship with the Father. One was to be humble and the other was to be obedient in all things.

Further discussion:
- Consider the description of the heart of Lucifer, wvho became Satan, in Isaiah 14:12-15. What are indications of pride and rebellion (or disobedience) in him?
- Read the book of Jonah. What examples can you see of God extending mercy when there had been disobedience? What caused God to be merciful?
- There are many benefits ascribed in the Bible to humility. Consider the following passages. 1Kings 21:29, Psalm 9:12, Ps 25:9, Proverbs 3:34, Proverbs 11:2, Proverbs 29:23, Isaiah 29:19, Isaiah 57:15, Matthew 23:12, James 4:6

CHAPTER TWELVE

Does God Know My Name?

I want to finish with one more thought and that pertains to having vision for our future. Sometimes our walk is lonely, the path seems dark, and we cannot see how it will end. Perhaps the Lord has given us a promise or promises and there seems no hope of their coming to pass. Promises are conditional and normally their fulfillment is dependent on our actively seeking after God. In this discussion we shall assume that the delay in fulfilment is due to God's timing, not some discrepant behavior or attitude on our part.

There is a pertinent passage of the Bible that we should consider in regard to this predicament. In Psalm 105:19, speaking of Joseph we read, "Until the time that his word came to pass, the word of the Lord tested him." What does this mean? Joseph was given promises in dreams, that one day he would be elevated to a position of authority over his brothers and even his father. As the eleventh of twelve sons, this would never occur under normal circumstances in his day. We can wonder just what Joseph thought might be the fulfillment of his dreams but it is unlikely that he ever imagined that God would elevate him to the position of power that he eventually held in Egypt.

So, Joseph had a promise but initially, things looked very dark indeed. He unjustly became a prisoner in a foreign land with no way to defend himself. The only person on the face of the earth who cared about him was his father and his father thought he was dead. There was a period of time until "the word came to pass" when that very word, or promise, that God had given tested Joseph to his core. What would Joseph think of the nature of God? Would he believe that God was faithful, true, and able to change his circumstances? Was God's word something that could be relied upon? Did He notice events in the lives of individuals or was He too aloof? Was He trustworthy? We know that from one day to the next, Joseph was elevated from prisoner to Prime Minister in Egypt. The word of the Lord certainly came to pass but until it did, that very same word tested Joseph in his whole understanding of the nature of God.

I want to share a story to show the great love that God has for us, a love for individuals like you and me. One day, my wife and I were seated in church and a couple came in and sat in the row in front of us. It was obvious that something was greatly troubling the lady, and when the first song started and we all stood to praise and worship the Lord, instead of standing she slumped forward with her head in her hands. During the service, the Lord spoke to my wife, Jillian. He told her that the lady's name was Susan (I have used a fictitious name) and that she was to go to Susan and tell her that God knew her name and all of the details of the difficult circumstances in her life.

At the close of the service, with some trepidation, Jillian slipped into the seat beside the lady and asked, "Is your name Susan?" The lady looked surprised that a stranger would know her name but replied that it was, and so Jillian proceeded to tell Susan what the Lord had given her to say, that God knew her name and all the details of her life.

Susan looked at Jillian, utterly shocked, and then began to explain. Two days earlier, she and her husband had taken their daughter to an amusement park for their daughter's birthday. Susan had lupus and expected to be able to use a wheelchair but the park refused to allow her. She decided to proceed through the park on foot, knowing that she would suffer as a result, but she did not want to disappoint her daughter. Sure enough, by Sunday morning she was in great pain and it is a wonder that she came to church. As the music began, she slumped forward and said, "Lord, I am in such pain and it seems that You don't even notice."

"Do You see the things that happen in my life?"

"Do You even know my name?"

So our wonderful Heavenly Father told her name to a stranger so that Susan would always know that He cared about her and every detail of her life.

To continue to grow in our walk with the Lord is to come to know Him better. Like Susan, we find that He is kind and caring, full of the fruit of the Spirit that He wants us to reflect. As the apostle John wrote, "… God is light and in Him is no darkness at all" (1 John 1:5). No darkness, not even a shadow, completely pure, completely good, full of love, full of mercy. We have to place our trust in His unerring wisdom, assured that He is well able to perform what He promised. Our heart must be grounded in eternal matters, not the things of our brief life on Earth. As we allow Him to change us within, we exhibit more and more of His wonderful nature. And perhaps our fellowship with Him can become "an association of persons with similar tastes, a friendly relationship, companionship." A fellowship of friends.